RAND McNALLY
Deserts

A *Where Are We?* Book

by Chris Arvetis
and Carole Palmer

illustrated by James Buckley

**Rand McNally
for Kids™**
Books•Maps•Atlases

This is the biggest sand pile I've ever seen.
Where did it come from?

We're in a desert.
The largest desert in the world is the Sahara.
About one fifth of the land area of the earth is deserts.

Many of the world's deserts are found in two wide bands to the north and south of the equator. Some of the world's largest deserts are in this section: Sahara, Australian, Arabian.

Deserts are also found in areas of the world where mountains block the rainfall and cause the land on the other side to be very dry. The Great Basin Desert in Nevada, the Mojave in California, and the Patagonia in Argentina are examples.

Other deserts are along coastal areas. The cold ocean winds stop the moisture from reaching the land. The coastal desert in Baja California and the Atacama Desert in Chile and Peru are two examples.

Some people say that a place is a desert if it is very hot and gets very little rainfall.
Others say a desert must also have a dry type of soil where only certain special plants grow.

Hot, Hot, Hot!

The Gobi desert in China and Mongolia is another kind of desert. It is found inland; far away from any body of water. The Gobi is the third largest desert in the world.

The most amazing areas to be called deserts are the frozen tundra of the ice deserts. The frozen areas of the Arctic, Antarctica, and Greenland are examples of this kind of desert. It is the dry climate with little, if any, rainfall that makes these areas deserts.

We usually think of deserts as very hot places, but there are deserts that are very cold too. These are included as deserts because they get very little rainfall so that it is hard for anything to grow there.

We could use some rain.

In the ice deserts, it is extremely cold. It is difficult to survive the cold temperatures, but a few hardy plants and animals can be found.

Polar bear

Musk ox

Deserts are known for their sand. However, only a small part of a desert is sand. Mostly it is bedrock, gravel, boulders, and soil. Deserts also have *sand dunes,* which are shaped by the wind. They can be crescent shaped, sword shaped, or star shaped.

But, let's look at the deserts we know best—the hot ones! One thing we see is a lot of sand.

When the wind blows, it piles up the sand, and sand dunes are formed.

Dunes come in many shapes and sizes.

Giant sand mountains in the deserts of Saudi Arabia stand over 650 feet tall. Other dunes can be over 800 feet tall.

Besides sand, there is soil, gravel, boulders, and mountains.
There are flat-topped hills called *mesas* and smaller ones called *buttes*.

Interesting formations.

Sandstorms occur in the desert. Winds of more than ten miles an hour can blow the sand across the desert creating a cloud of sand. The sandstorms can blow sand over six feet high and last from three to five hours.

When the sun heats the air near the ground, a *dust devil* can be formed. Sand is picked up in the whirling column of air and tossed 1,000 or more feet above the earth.

Besides the sand, desert areas have many other interesting landforms. There can be mountain ranges, plateaus, plains, volcanic peaks, and unusual bedrock formations.

The amount of rainfall in a desert varies from year to year. In some deserts, several years can go by without rain. Then ten inches of rain can come down very quickly. Much of the rain does not soak into the ground.

Rain showers are always welcome in the desert. The chart gives the average yearly rainfall for specific places in the desert areas.

	Annual Precipitation
Mojave Desert, Nevada	4.01 in.
Atacama Desert, Chile	0.00 in
Sahara Desert, Algeria	3.02 in.
Alice Springs, Australia	9.92 in.
McMurdo, Antarctica	3.97 in.

Even though it is dry on the land, deserts always have an underground water supply. Wells are drilled so that water can be brought up to use for people and animals as well as for watering (irrigating) crops.

The heat and the lack of water make life in the desert difficult. In North America, desert dwellers often live in adobe or mud houses. These houses keep out the heat and hot sun.

The water runs rapidly down the hillsides following the dried up streams.
As the water runs, it carries along gravel, rock, and sand.
When the stream gets to the bottom, it drops the sand and rocks in a big, fan-shaped area.

In Africa and Asia, desert dwellers move from place to place in search of water and land to use for grazing their herds. The people live in tents and wear long robes to protect themselves from the wind and heat.

The mountain streams can also carry the rainfall into dry lake beds called *playas*.
For a while, a lake is formed. Then the water soaks into the ground or goes back into the air.
Eventually, the lake dries up again.

A process called *erosion* is always at work in the desert. The rare rainstorms, strong winds, and blowing sand wear away the rock formations and change the landscape.

Monument Valley in Arizona shows wind erosion with the resulting towering rock formations. Water erosion can be seen in the Namib Desert in Africa where rock walls have been built to stop water erosion.

Deserts can have a green
area where plants grow
and people settle.
This area is called an *oasis*.
An underground stream, spring,
or well supplies water so that the
trees, shrubs, and grasses grow.
People also make artificial oases
by drilling wells and using the
water to irrigate their crops.

The word *desertification* is used to tell how desert
areas are spreading into new areas. People, climate,
or a combination of the two have turned good land
into eroding deserts.

In the Sahara, two thirds of the people live by the oases and depend on wells for watering their crops. The date palm is the main food for these people. Some cereals, apricots, peaches, citrus fruits, and figs are grown in the shaded areas.

Of all the desert plants, the cactus is one of the most well-known of all desert plants. Look at all the kinds of cactus.

Saguaro

Special plants and animals grow in the desert.
Everyone knows about the cactus plants.
These plants can live in a dry, hot climate.
The stems store water to use during the very dry times.
Look at all the different kinds of cactus plants.

Ouch!

Prickly pear Barrel cactus Hedgehog cactus Pincushion cactus

Those roots go way down.

I know!

In the southwestern United States, the mesquite trees have long roots that go deep into the ground to find water. The roots can go forty feet down into the Earth.

Some deserts have plants that grow flowers.

After a rainfall, the plants quickly bloom and turn the desert into a beautiful sight.

Desert flowers can live without water for months. Some have a lot of roots that find all the water in the soil. Others like cactuses, can store water in their stems to use during dry spells. All of these desert flowers can be seen in North American deserts.

California poppy

Arizona lupine

Sand verbena

Wild zinnia

Many of the animals that live in the desert can survive for days without water.

Some of them dig down into the ground while others look for shade under trees and rocks.

Many animals stay out of the sun during the day and search for food and water at night.

The diagram shows how many desert creatures burrow into the ground to keep away from the heat. Some of these animals sleep during the summer while it is so very hot.

Kit fox

Bull snake

Kangaroo rat   Pocket mouse   Trap-door spider   Horned lizard   Ant lion

Insects, spiders, snakes, lizards, scorpions, and tortoises are found in most deserts.
Common birds such as wrens, quails, woodpeckers, and sparrows can be seen as well as hawks, eagles, vultures, and roadrunners.

I'm in a hurry.

Desert animals are adapted to the desert heat and short supply of water. Lizards, scorpions, insects and spiders have thick skin to stop water loss. Bird's feathers help keep them cool. Some animals can live off the water they get from plants and seeds.

1 lizard	6 woodpecker
2 scorpion	7 hawk
3 tortoise	8 eagle
4 wren	9 vulture
5 quails	10 roadrunner

9

8

4

6

5

2

Hummingbird

Elf owl

Swallowtail
butterfly

Gila monster

Mice, hares, rabbits, and kangaroo rats are typical small desert animals.

Mule deer, coyotes, antelopes, and bobcats are some of the larger desert animals.

I just want a small bite.

The people of Africa and Asia depend on camels to help with the work, to supply food, and to use for transportation. Camels can walk across the deserts and go for long periods of time without water. They store fat for food in the hump on their back.

1 mouse
2 rabbit
3 coyote
4 antelope
5 kangaroo rat
6 mule deer
7 bobcat

Arabian camel

Bactrian camel

Many deserts have deposits of oil and natural gas which makes the land very valuable. Besides all the unusual landforms and strange creatures deserts are interesting sights.